Loving Bloom
By
Marinela Domingos

First Edition, 2024.

Mande Imperio

Luanda, Angola

www.mandewomen.com

Dedications

To my younger self, who desperately wanted to become

A published author, I hope I made you proud.

To my beautiful and loving family and friends your support and

affection for me really increased my courage to keep going, thank
you.

This book was written for every word, thought and

unspoken feelings. I tried to bring to light what we fear

 sharing, just to let you know that you are not alone and that

it's okay to feel your emotions.

With love, Nela.

Table of Contents

Stained Mirror

It's become obvious,

My need,

To please your every hidden thought

Granting me permission

To be pleased with myself

I find myself observing

What gives your eyes pleasure

What gives your thoughts measure

What values you treasure

My pretence exceeds me

It's become too cocky

I must enclose

Though I may be considered an art

My procrastination smudges me

A zodiac trait as you so passionately stated

There's no longer an instance

Where I write

And not find ridicule in the alphabet

It's as though I write for you

My muse

But your sophistication

Your maturity

Have gifted you with the finest palate

Rendering my work that of an imbecile

A failed attempt at impressing you

When I should be loving you

I digress

I compared my works to your being

And I met death

At the gates of heaven

Holding pieces written by yours truly

Set ablaze by my trait

Heated Consequence

I despise my rage toward you

Makes me miss you more

I want to hate you but a sudden thirst for your

fingertips on my back condemns me

An exhausting hunger to be in your presence

makes haste to weaken me

I hear your voice in my imaginations of me

screaming at you

Lips quiver in hopes that you'll sting them

Fingers tremble in hopes that you'll embalm them

with yours

I want to beat at your beautiful chest but my ears

yearn to hear your irregular heartbeat

I don't want to look into your eyes

That's how my rage dissolves

Being angry at you makes me love you

An almost tangible love

That makes me feel the weight of my spirit beneath

my flesh

My fury makes sets me ablaze for you

And when you roll your sleeves to handle me

When you're angry and your veins are exposed

When you're less vocal and more physical

I crave you

The Covenant

I am wasting your time

As you wait so patiently for me to bloom

I engage in mental activities of comparison to your

accolades in human form

I am selfish for questioning your choice in me

I can't help it, what do I have to give?

My lack is bigger than my potential

It's evident in how I love you with fear

How I love you like a religion

Trying to be the perfect sum of all your past and

present lovers

All the souls blessed by your loyalty

I am exhausted

I was stronger in my younger years than I am now

I suffer from a bitterness bred from my blindness to

myself

I love you like a religion

So attached

Holding on for dear life with no life in it

I'm an empty vessel attempting to fill myself up

with you

Limited Edition

I've been filled with this loving excitement to share myself with you.

Not physically as we do so passionately and not emotionally as it was on demand.

I want to do it entirely in a non-romantic sense, in a more in control and willing way.

I have all of this beauty in me and I want you to experience it, taste it, sip it, observe it, indulge in it, paint in it, overwhelm yourself in it, calm down in it, and grow with and in it.

I'm excited to introduce the version of me that cracked the stone shell.

I want to introduce her to you by baptizing you in me.

I'm excited to bring together all my wisdom and discernment,

My acceptance and boundaries, my value and

worth, my time and presence,

My aura and gift, my godly relationship,

my divinity,

My shortcomings, my apologies and generosity,

My travels and dishes, my scents and my new

body.

Dreamer

I look forward to inspiring you,

Making you laugh,

Filling your belly,

Bathing with you around the world,

Taking walks around the world,

Inviting things and people into our experiences,

Being walking passions together.

I look forward to watching the flowers drool over

us,

The birds dance over us, the earth slow down over

us.

I look forward to learning

Because I feel everything and everyone that has

Been here before, are here and are on their way

have so much to teach.

It's a patient honeycomb hunger I've got for life.

I feel still, like I'm floating with purpose.

I'm excited to share my writings and newly

accumulated thoughts,

Thoughts brought forward from my time in life's

Womb.

I'm excited to be your muse in a different angle.

I'm excited to paint and sketch with you.

I'm excited to shop for furniture and statues with

you.

I'm excited to be part of your new journey in my

wholeness, to be so present and aware that my

hairs stand.

I'm excited to love you.

I'm excited to share my being, my core, my foetus,

my soul, with you

Yours

Pardon my immaturity

I want to be all the joys you've had

Pardon my selfishness

I want to be all you need

I wish I was the first girl you smelled

The first young woman to catch your eye

Your first kiss

I wish I was the first woman to use you

The first female body you worshipped

The first to show you what a woman is

And how to treat one

I wish I was your first fling

Your first love

The first to make you feel like a man

I wish I was your first whore

The first girl or woman to wink at you

The first woman whose hugs gave you goose

bumps

The first woman to respect you

Though my jealousy consumes me

My loyalty inspires me

To make every moment with you a first

Besides, I am here now

I'm my own woman, with you

Pessimist

All these years, all these experiences, all the advice and observations have amounted to questions upon questions.

It's never been said in the history of mankind, that one has loved wrong.

Most would pride themselves in the knowledge that they are the first at something but what about when they are the first to love wrong?

How does a woman orchestrate her fantasies into her reality?
It's strange to find yourself in a position that requires the integration and elimination of identity, almost novelist to the eyes of a blooming teenage girl.

How beautiful was sacrifice to me.

A security found in the distant possibility of

someone giving their all for you.

Desires for long adorning stares and tear absorbing

kisses.

A scorching thirst for acknowledgement and

approval from your dear sweet love.

Suddenly the record scratches, new compositions

are introduced.

A more oriented and sophisticated sonata.

The guitar no longer whirls through memories, it

pauses between the piano and base.

The vocals get deeper and drums slow down.

What now?

Golden

Solitude and proof of worthiness becomes high in demand. Freedom of eccentric expression is reduced in supply.

Romance becomes a fatality. Dreams become subtle compromises.

I don't know how to love you mature. I take no pride in my infantile deficiency. I'm learning to work around my romantic calamities.

Can you see my eyes crack like a rock under pressure, ready to pave new ways for waves?

I used to look at flowers with adoration, now I see them as aliens unknown to the senses.

To neglect a love you dreamt of for the sake of growth baffles me.

I don't know how to say I miss you, I love you, without saying it.

Is the composure in a woman a cover for grief of lost fairy tales? Is the confidence of a woman a boundary?

Don't they hold the hands of their lover idly stroking each knuckle? Don't they watch their partner adoringly talk about their passions?

Don't they want to shower their partner with kisses and hugs?

Don't they want to amuse their partner to tears?

Don't they seek comfort in the arms of their

partner?

How does a grown woman love?

What Are You Thinking?

That's the unfair advantage you have over me

You can read me but I can't read you

I can dream

I can wonder

… Assume

But never know

You can tell me what you're thinking

What you're feeling

I still won't know

Cause your words are poetic

Poetic stings

They slice

Call it what, traumatic?

I like that

We know that's what made me

We know that's what invades you

Is this dark?

Can't call it a colour because it hasn't any

We created a world

And to the world it is a black and white silent

movie

To me it's a never lived before aspired enigma

But…

What are you thinking?

Dear Beloved

I don't argue in person but I fight you in poems

I press the pen so hard scratching your chest

Strike a line through words that you can't hear me

say in my head

Flip the page so violently to push you through the

wall

Make my handwriting smaller to scream at you

Add no title so you know to read my mind

Piece words together carefully like my hips move

to your thrusts

Devote my emotion to the pen like I do to your

being

Bend the rules of literature like we bent the rules on

age

Burn the page with ink as we did outsiders

opinions on us

Write letters in my head you've never read, same

way you tell me I love you

Calm my words down like you do when you touch

me... With your presence

End the poem abruptly to disconnect

Cause I can't argue with you

But my silent words do

They just never get to you

But my eyes expose my truth

I'm desperately in love with... *sigh

Closet

You care so much you hurt me with the words of a
healer and a master. You've made me feel small
and I've become accustomed to that loving
aggression.

I'm not a victim, just a sensitive learner. Good
teachers don't say much but when they do, we
listen. I've learnt a lot from you which has boiled
down to one thing, experience is not an ego boost,
it humbles you.

My being feels tossed in a bowl of steel sitting on
fire when I hear your corrections.

You care, that's why it hurts. I can't not show my

gratitude for your effortless efforts yet why say

thank you when there's a "but" right after?

My perception of life and who I am feels trivial.

Even my poetic skills have toned down to

accommodate my rather narrow opinions.

The more I learn from you the more I wonder

whether I am fit for this world. It's as raw as you

are. Unpredictable as you are. Cold as you can be.

Sharp as you are. Punishing as you can be.

What can a sensitive young lady do in a world as

such? Learn. All I can really do is learn. I learn from

you every day.

I learn about myself when I am with you. I learn

about you. You are not nice, you're honest.

I don't need nice, I was nice for two decades and

where has that gotten me? Crying in my bedroom

corner because you corrected me because you care

about me… And it hurt me.

Threesome

What one would call a liberated woman danced in

front of me smiling, laughing, swinging her eyes

and rotating her free hips.

I watched her, smiling at her own creation. An

elegant figure with more than enough desire to

intoxicate men of war and religious women.

Her breasts wink at me while the silhouette of her

dance stroked my masculinity.

Well-travelled and well-read, this woman. A free

spirit trapping and controlling noble men.

She was the focus in this dim lit planet where men

spread their legs to allow room for pulsation while

I crossed my legs providing a seat for her bare

honour.

I wanted to kiss her, smell her and taste her. I
wanted to be inside her while she blossoms
allowing room for depth.

But instead I let you indulge in her while I watched
seated between her hips.

Royalty

Like Makeda, I rule my kingdom. Planning in
silence and delegating myself on my own. Like
Makeda, it's uncertain whether I have fallen for
your pleasantries or challenge your complexities, I
need none.

Walking through boulevards of my world I
discovered: solace upon a mountain of love,
streams of reverence from my river to your fever,
roots synched to yours and mind subconscious,
winds travelling with luggage of past lives and
whispers enabling me to hew the present.

No statues in my world, memories should be set
free and not temporarily frozen in time. Blankets of

snow cover our mountainous shields. We're story

tellers of times unsealed.

Rain is unannounced; its scent lures you to my

presence anew. The best way to love you, as

Makeda did Solomon.

Quietly gaze into your power, heightening your

guard, become subject to my wisdom as a symbol

of my naked curves and luscious pubes.

To walk and talk into your kingdom with my

highness and bow to the greatness of your mother's

waters.

Crawl into the cave of your subdued discretions

keeping company to the man you call a monster

within. Caress you when you're angry and

meditate upon your joys. Tell stories to your hair
and recite poems on your skin.

I, Makeda, water you. My spices are luxurious but
my womb runs deep in her essence loving your
solitude.

Pleasure

A high on a reality that is questionable

Left to play lucidly

Memories have no hold on re-living moments

Barriers of time irrelevant to the feeling

Being seeing breathing

Smoking baking dreaming

Never asleep only humming

Concrete floors and desert sands, old friends

Cigar and whiskey scents display my paintings

Sweat from the saxophone hold credit to my

writings

Luminous nights on another earth

Nostalgic present day

Dancing my life away

Into another day

Through portals of trumpets and memories

Miles into serenity

I'm high off my melody

Jazzy things I do to me

Every evening

Would you dare to see?

Jealous

The nights are the hardest

Because you love yourself

You go to sleep peacefully

While I battle my demons

Hoping you'll reach out

Knowing that you won't

Now I curse self-love

It takes you away

From loving me

Though my misery

Marital Seduction

My passions betray my clarity

When we engulf ourselves in the throes of passion

Found myself longing for your otherness

To overthrow my desires

Your gentleness gives me great pleasure yet

Inner flames sizzle for your dark veins

Is it betrayal if I long for your otherness?

Is it confusion if I want your Gemini

simultaneously?

Shall I label myself a swinger with one lover to

swing and dual passions to thrill?

When I kiss your upper lip

I am devoured by your lower

When I caress your swollen chest,
Your back grows bolder
Your strokes grow gentler
But my fire, stronger

Ironically,
When your darkness feasts upon me
I search for your dignity
I find it watching me, in pain
As I express my ache in multitudes
I find your heart apologizing for your coldness

There is loyalty to our love
But I cannot help but lust
Over your ego

Chaos

I believe it apt to say

Monogamy is an act of the ego

Polygamy a character of the spirit

Because soul mates can be more than one

But, how does one share a soul mate

Without losing one?

How do I share you, without losing me?

How do I share your vulnerability?

Knowing another soul has access

To corners I probably don't know of?

My qualifications seem limited for your

requirements

I know you to a certain degree

I honour your intellect

I've mastered your desires

I've doctored your darkness

Yet the realms of the cosmos

Betray my naivety

There is no one soul mate

But there is...

There is a needy soul with recycled slates

For the evenings where you wake

To my face

Desiring a different embrace

It's where I quake

Virgin

What is it that makes my love for you, necessary?

Is it your mystery, which tickles my insomnia?

Your confidence, which weds my insecurity?

Perhaps the question isn't clear

Is my love, for you?

Or for my need for a tangible purpose?

Am I circling around my embarrassment?

My wondering pond ponders upon

The real question

Which questions my truth

Is my love necessary for you?

Food for Thought

Love dies from the obsession over the thought that

love can never die

Famine

Will your lips bid me undone?

May I whisper into your lungs?

The mysteries of what I've become

Shall we whimper into the abyss?

Granting my woman zest to set you free

Let my maturity persuade your greed

Perhaps redirect your beastly needs to me

Opposites Attract

I have detached my female desires

To accommodate my feminine sensibility

To suit the likes of your society

To suit the likes of your lifestyle

My back is straight

My thoughts are silenced

The evening is graced

With your manner…

Of conquering me my foolishness

Exposing my submissive nature

Mirroring my lustful fears

You've stoked my comfort zone

Only to elate my inner disease

Kept at bay, even from me

I'll allow my conscience to grieve

The possibilities of our delicate atrocities

Our adventures

Our proximity

Our love

If we were not denied

The freedom of being accessories

To our beloved complexities

Trophy

I fight you in my weakness

So desperate to be grounded

I see you as my enemy

My enemy who protects me

My expectations blind my reasoning

I'm found packing away my maturity

To rely on your wisdom

To surrender to your sensibility

But still wounded by my dependence

I find the need to prove to you

That I don't need you

Revealing just how much I do

I'm still acquiring my independence

But every inch I get

I give to you

By hoping that you see me

The same way you see

Your accolades

Sundays at 5pm

Autumn has come

Falling leaves announce my arrival

A graceful entrance publicly discrete

Grey lines and short speech

Fountain pens and long nights

A human blend of red wines

Let's create love, this time

Though my youth was bright

My light is dim

Accommodating your senses

Celebrating Elohim

Surely my independence won't spite you

My loneliness inspire you

My thunder entice you

My scents will never leave your subconscious

I have turned you to poetry

The sweet perfume of life

Intoxicating every line

With sprays of your wooden rhythm

An immortal library, that you are

I will be your Sunday, personified

Grown

My smooth face fades

Shiny hair dulls

And charm deepens

At the mercy of my last strings of youth

A youth external and shy

Daring but careful

Fearful but kind

Creatively naive

I fear becoming a memory

But time is at cost

Forgive my immaturity

I must grieve this art

My older self is a mystery

I hope she compliments your vice

May you want her as bad

May you want her as deep

I can't help but fear

Her wisdom erase me

Her demeanor evade me

And her presence degrade me

Remember me when you laugh with her

But that too would be an ache for her heart

It's a silly thought to have

And yet, I wonder

Will you love her more than you love me?

Will you pay me a visit while she sleeps?

Will you hear my cries when she swallows her

tears?

Will you notice my desperation in her fears?

Lover,

Will you still water me?

Food for Thought

How could you ask for a perfect ending

When not all poems rhyme?

Imagination

I love you like a memory

Distant but so personal

Faint yet clear

Quiet but strongly scented

In the past, but futuristic

Sober

Let us take a walk down the avenues less visited by

the tongues of amateur lovers.

I am one of them, no better than an orphan.

When will we realize that it is the person that must

be loved and not what stands between them?

Let us unpack the questions not asked for fear of a

bad reaction.

Let's unfold the doubts and assumptions left quiet

because they feed the loneliness that comes with

unannounced separation within a union.

Let's remove the stitches from hurtful exchange of

words.

Let's expose the hidden expectations built from

our inner child's fairytales.

Let's wring the flesh of its unattended tactile

desires.

Let's stretch the lungs to exhale all sighs of ignored

signs for affection.

Let's inspect the ears for misunderstandings.

Let's expand the eyes to strip the held back tears

from moments in which one broke down before

their lover, undetected.

Now we reach the end of the road.

Bare, exposed, open stitches, frail bones, cold skin

and bloody tears.

A shaky voice and mass fear.

Vulnerable and cornered.

Imperfections revealed.

Ribs ruptured; there is no protecting the heart.

Slow and steady palpitations.

Tiresome breathing, eyes half shut.

These are the unexplored avenues.

This is where we love from.

The Sting Of Alchemy

I envy my future self

She gets the applause for the work I'm putting in

She gets to sleep peacefully because I undergo the

teary nights

She's comfortable with who she is, while I question

my worth as a spirit

As a woman

I over think and she gets to execute

She drinks green tea in Japan while I salivate my

self defence

I envy my future self

She is loved by her spirit

She is whole by herself

She is humble though accomplished

I want to make myself worthy

She bathes elegantly in her worth

Through every season and era

She sees beneath the beauty of all under the moon

While I am patted on the back for my silence

I envy my future self

She is complimented on her freedom

And I for my resilience

I envy my future self

She has her own world and lives in it gracefully

She knows who she is

I envy the love I will have for myself in the future

I envy my future self

Cause she's already loved by you

Mirror Mirror

When you said goodnight

That's when I felt it

A ray of insignificance

A solitude that tickles emotional intelligence

Awareness as bitter as empty vengeance

A longing deeper than regret

It's not my music I must face at night

It is the lyrics I must embrace

So once you say goodnight

My orchestra takes flight

The bow strikes and cuts

Drums hit and crush

Strings strum a screech

Trumpets blow off tune

The silence ensues

And the lyric subdues

Alone you are, the night is due
I've come to ask one thing of you
Forgive yourself for aching through
The years of youth with pleasant truths
Alone you are, the night is due
I've come to ask one thing of you
Embrace the karma that comes with guilt
Embrace the love that comes with filth
Celebrate the nights of dancing tears
Show love and care to your deepest fears

When you said goodnight is when I felt it
A ray of insignificance...

Confidential

Sensitive…

Silk dipped in a pool of milk

A pearl dripping urges

Ruby's active in my center

Diamonds melting in my cum

Gold bleeding through my ears

Fireworks cracking me open

Iron surrendering through my eyes

Fire cupping my breasts

A circle of lightning wringing my hips

Titanium enlightens my throat

Cumulus clouds guard my waist

Sunlight glows below me

My waves are erupting volcanoes

Tectonic plates are trembling

My core isn't contained

My weather is changing

Mars has fallen

Venus rules

She's ruthless with her love

Gentle with her bruise

In my longing for your honor

I took a walk in the unexplored seas

A tear dropped and humanity faded

And in that moment I felt you rise

I felt you rule

I felt you true

I needed you

So I wiped out everyone that wasn't you

Nothing they say is true

For love isn't blind when I can see your truth

Love isn't blind if you can see my bruise

Love isn't blind if it loves us too

Look, my portal is open

Sink into me my love

Listen to the soaked calling of your name

Listen to the wet pat singing to your mouth

Look into my velvet opening

Dive into me, samurai

Let us explode together

Let's make love to our passion

Like fallen angels with humans

This is my madness

For you...

Eat me

I'll quench your thirst

I am your monsoon

Patience

I don't want to let go.

This is all I know.

I don't want to let go of the fact that you're the most

important person in my life.

I don't want to stop thinking only about us and our

future together I don't want to make anything

separate.

To me it's just you and I and I don't want to let go

of that.

Please understand me.

I waited long...

So long to find you

I long to be with you which is yet another wait

Something in me wants me to stop putting our love
on top and make room for more but I am scared.
Our love is the most special thing I have and know
to be true.

I confess that I do obsess over us because it's the
one thing that saved me. I understand that I am not
letting go forever and simply making room for
more but I just can't.
All my inspiration comes from us
My strength, my drive and the main reason I'm
doing my best at trying to be patient… it's for us to
be together.

U-turn

I fear what could happen to this version of me

I'm not sure how to move on from the version of

me that is bleeding.

I've done everything I can.

From Jesus to Buddha to ancestors to the universe

to God...

Yet I still sit with this bitterness and fear.

My confusion exhausts me and gets me angry

Even when I do what the universe requires even

when I don't control anything, the dagger just

keeps digging deeper

I'm in the in between

Between life and death and both are calling me

I don't know who I'll be but I know I'll be even

more vulnerable

I'm scared

I don't want the universe to be right

For once I want to be right

I want to feel like I know what's best for me and let

it be true because all my life I've been proven

wrong

It's been a long fight and I'm tired...

I just want to be right

Not better, just right

I just want to be with you

Saudade

The things I do when I miss you

I hug myself and wake up with my spirit inside

you

I think back to our memories like a vintage

documentary

I think of our future like I envy how we're living so

happily

I look at my hands and I feel yours on my lips

I bite my bottom lip and feel you breathe through

my skin

I look around and see you everywhere

I plan little trips and tricks to explore

I think about to satisfy you even more

I write books to you

I talk to you

I even get high on my feelings for you

That I start hallucinating about universal versions

of you

The greatest things that I do for you

Is work on myself to be better for you

I can't wait till you witness my heart in real time

I found my purity and I've become a real dime

I miss you boo

Blink

I often wonder why people think romance is the absence of life. Saying "you are my air" seems so cliché, mundane... Boring. It's better to want something rather than to dismiss its importance entirely.

You... You make me want to breathe a little deeper, to feel a little deeper, to see a little deeper and to dive a little deeper into myself. You make me want to be here, remain here. You make me want to be loved by you. And I enjoy it. Every second of it.

Divine

Forgive me for my doubts over your love for me

But the love you give is too pure for this world

So I wonder, with my sins, am I deserving of your

love?

Why would a divine man love me so much?

I hid parts of me from myself

I ran away from them hoping to be someone else

Your curiosities lead you in deep

You got to know the parts of me I'm afraid of

Without judgment, without fear

You touched every part of me with your gentleness

Now every single part of me yearns for your touch

From my darkness to my light to my unhealed trust

How can a man like you love a woman like me?

Not only that but you're so loyal to me

Perhaps this is what all religions fail to see

A love so Godly

A love that saved me

A love that healed me

Setting me free

First Class

Cheers and gratitude

To the afternoon I run into your arms with scents of

an air plane's window seat

To our first night and day alone painting the skies

alive

To the spontaneous nights of travels and random

drinking sessions

To the restaurant and bar dates soaked in sparkling

eyes and formal gestures

To opening envelopes from God bearing great

news of our friendship's deeds

To long nights of laughter, pizza and wine

To trying new things together and laughing at each

other

To supporting one another through the trials and

through the breeze

To teaching and learning one another as we grow

To milestones decorating our hearts

To serious moments centered in trust and loyalty

To commitment birthed from our deepest intimacy

To being children together and having them too

To building a home, our heaven, our bloom

To celebrations in abundance

To drunk dance moves and high conversations

To being intoxicated by one another

To our passion

To our drive

To our ambition

To our lives

To a new beginning at last

You are my home, meu amor

The echoes of our love

Sail me back to you

Food for Thought

How simple it is to love you

That I may break before your eyes unnoticed

Tempted to ask if you do not see the fire drowning

in my teary red eyes

But one knows better than to question the sight of a

seer.

Champion

So proud of your accolades

They represent you well

You strut at the thought of them

You've done well for yourself

Your confident arrogance gleams through your sly

smirk

Claims are that you're trying to inspire me

Comes off as mockery

They are some of your best work, these accolades

You show them off like a proud father

They're you're girls as you've said

Your soul mates as you've professed

So what am I?

A high school prize giving certificate?

I crave the effort you put into displaying your

accolades

I wish you put that effort into nurturing my silent

needs

Nature

Under the orange sun

The dust, swift with its passing

The morning sun is a sad melody

To awaken to the absence of my lover

To awaken to the longing of his heat

My cup fails to warn me

Before I know it my insides melt

Reminding me of how I felt

Whenever he'd smile at me

Look at me

Touch me

If missing you is a disease

Then mine has become chronic

Petite

Why do I love you

Is it because I'm desperate for affection

Because I long for warm attention

Is it because of how I didn't grow up

Or because I'm not good enough

Is it because your eyes light up when you see me

Or that my illusions delude me

Is it because of how you perceive me

Or because of how I wish I could see me

Is it because you make the truth sound pretty

Or because lies have comfortably invaded me far

too long

Is it because I want to be a specific woman

Or because I want to be your woman

Is it due to lack

Or an influx

Is it because melanin glows better when in love

Or because my letters build synagogues

Is it because my petite compliments your greatness

Or because maturity is a rare jewel

Do I love you as an extension of me

Or do I love you within me

Do I love you as a man

Do I love you as a God

Oh I love you like a prayer

I love you like a fast

I love you because I've lived without you

And I no longer want that

Immortal

Loving me must be difficult

I know this because loving you is so easy

From a smiley face

And bright energy

To ions of frustration

And sad energy

You smile at me hoping I'll feel better

But my biggest sin is the control my emotions have

on me

You water my garden and provide sufficient light

Yet I present you with a desert

You pump my heart with genuinity

And I sing the sad violin

I'm sorry

My lack of balance

I'm crippled

But sometimes I think it's optional

Though I'm programmed to self –destruct

Thoughts of you impede such actions

I see you through my fog

I hear you in my mists

I reach out to you through withdrawals

My blank expressions are an overwhelming

amount of tears

My sudden absence is a cry for your attention

I used to turn to music for consolidation

But everyone seems to be in love

Or in deep hate

But I simply want you here

Come smile

Or tears

Stab

They say that to love others

We must love ourselves first

But how is it that I detest my essence

I cannot stand my desires

And my needs are but a desperate cry for pity

Yet I looked you in the eyes

I spoke to your soul

I connected to who you were in the beginning of

time

And I declared to you

That I love you

And I repeated it

With each stab

Which each punch

With each strike of your ego

I love you,

Is this self sabotage?

Cocky

So…here we are

Strangers again

Except we're strangers that have tasted each others sins

Strangers with a missing piece

I'm strained, as I watch you

Forcing the love you feel for me, to transform into hate

Perhaps I'm ugly in your eyes

But you see, I always told you how unattractive I am

It's the river on my thighs that lathered you with lust

My breasts hypnotized you into pouring your honey in my cave

It was my rapid paced heart that fooled your ears

I knew that I was ugly to your eyes

Now that it's no longer something you hide

I'd like to know, did you take a look inside?

Though your charm is beaming externally

I made love to the venom you harbor within

It is the most hideous part of you that I became
vulnerable to

And now, now that a man loves me for my
unattractiveness

You still humble me with your poison

I thought the devil was a monster

But the night you submerged into my red river

In the back seat of your car

Parked in a common street

The night you sank your teeth into my plump fruit

And my juices rebelled down your lips

The night I drank your wine from the bottle

The night we embraced like fallen angels

The night I gushed while seated on your temple

Was the night we conceived the devil

It's no wonder we have so much in common

Ponder

What do you do

When memories become distant echoes

Drifting in your conscious like dreams

That you long to come true

What do you do

When they become whispers

Provoking your sense of hope

Lucid Feelings

I kissed my lover once,

On the day of his death

He was a warm man

He wouldn't let me die

But I'd kill myself for him

His eyes were the windows of angels

He was better than the heaven he came from

I counted the flowers we stole from time

When we'd sneak glances and slight- brushes from
thumb to brow

After dawn, our thoughts would create the music
of lovers

Our feelings would engage in passion

Our tears moistened our truth

That I shared his love with his wife

Though it felt like he had two

A noble man with a humble spirit

His presence, like the voices of sunsets by the river

So great was he., that his creator called early

The gates opened, like his arms in my embrace

The light drew him in just like his voice would to
my skin

He turned back to me with my tears in his palm

I thrust against him for the last touch

His eyes pierced my grief

His assurance melted my fear

He held, oh he held my spirit

I was ready for my depart

For life without him, is lifeless

He poured his last breath into me

And with that last breath, I tasted him for the first
time

He let go as the light praised him

We sat by the river and cried, like sisters

We grieved my lover

We grieved my friend

I kissed my lover once…

On the day of his death

Food for Thought

It is in the illusion of ego

That our flaws are introduced

Weak

Patience,

My biggest downfall

If not my enemy

An enemy that does me god

An ointment if I may

Ot's no surprise that I've always needed it

But first, I must learn it

What a battle it's been

But you've held my hand through it

You taught me to walk when I'd forget my pace
and sprint

I'm more than one person

But I'm aligned when I'm with you

My thoughts cease and together we embrace you

Your delicacy in reading my emotions

In feeling the needs of my soul

Your gentle gaze awakening the forgotten within
me

Your patience while I learn to be patient

Your kindness when I am cruel to myself

It's as they say "love is patient, love is kind"

I'm sorry but, I will boast of the way you love me

And though I promised to be patient while waiting
for our time

I tend to rush into our future

Loving me is not an easy climb

But we hike together

You lead me to my true self when I am blind

You truly are one of a kind

Mermaid

The sun sends waves of love

Penetrating my skin

My body shimmers and glows

Excreting bottled desires

Disguised as pearls of sweat

The heat is intense and comforting

Like the womb of a blooming mother

My lips are softer

But my thirst grows fonder

For waters I have yet to sip

And journeys I'm due to imbibe

As the rays submerge, it feels like an everlasting

kiss

Sure to leave permanent strokes

As the clouds surround it's glory

Creating quite the scenery

Even the birds have desires

Wings swaying provocatively

Like the eyes of a mistress in love

A great secret disguised in plain sight

A love story about the skies

Wound

My agony seeks refuge

Found in the darkest corner of silence

Eyes quake

Even my sleep betrays me

With the ghost of you

You may still be breathing

But

It is your touch, smile and scent

That dug a six feet whole inside me

Instead of roses, they threw nonchalance

Instead of hymns

I had echoes

Linen Sheets

It was a lustful insanity

The kind that tends to addiction

Almost like a fantasy

Captivated by your circumstance

Except, it wasn't a circumstance

You were content, fulfilled

The norm is to sing the boring pitiful hymn

"Why?"

What's fun is that I know why

I always knew why

When you thought you won

That you had the upper hand

I was in control

You served me your weakness

On a silver platter

That being my firm legs spread wide before you

And like a beast

I ravaged and clawed through it

Dissecting your bland ego

See, I'm a great enemy to trauma

But to manipulation, I am a nemesis

Cause I'm familiar with its work

And if I have mastered the destruction of a
sightless weapon

Who do you think you are to me?

A man? How lamentable

I remember you said you'd use me, eat me

But darling I don't eat, I feast

Your lust was used to your defeat

Selfless Ecstacy

Tell me something darling

Has it ever crossed your mind how I'd like to be
loved?

Do you not consider my nose worthy of the scent of
flowers?

Are petals not worthy of my joy?

Have you ever wondered if I am satisfied?

Do you really know how to love me

Have you tried to understand the impact your gaze
has upon me?

Was there ever

Stuck in time

If ever you wonder
This is what I'd like to hear from you
"Your care for me has eliminated my ear of
vulnerability
Your touch sparks the protective side of me
And gives me goosebumps
Your smile makes me warm
And your giggles put my troubles to rest
The scent of your hair surpass all gardens
Your skin, as soft as cotton
Your hugs are like a dream come true
Your mind is as complex as the stars we haven't
dared to see
And your spirit is quiet and filled with love
Your eyes are as mysterious as the rings of Saturn"
This is how I wish you viewed me
But from your words, all I am to you
Is a broken clock
A wasted potential
A failed promise
And crushed expectation

Fallen

Its never enough

Your eyes will always wonder off

Even though you said you like that I am natural

Your eyes still salivate when a woman crosses your
path

Perhaps I am to blame

I am the one who is insecure

That's why I try to please you even when I don't
feel like it

It's why I try to tend to your every need

But yet, you close your eyes and play with your
desires

While I lay asleep beside you

You've captured plenty of images with your mind

I can only imagine the scenes that aid your self
pleasure

No matter what I do

It's never enough

So why should I keep trying…

Relentless

I'm sorry

That I don't inspire you

I'm sorry I only have one perfume and it's
inexpensive

I'm sorry I lack luxury

My speech isn't pristine and I'm sorry I don't like
going out much

I'm sorry my hair doesn't smell like mangoes nor
does it look perfect all the time

I'm sorry I get my period cause you can't get your
pleasures

I'm sorry I'm not as ambitious as the women you
encounter

I'm sorry by butt isn't as big as my friends'

I'm sorry I don't cook or clean like your mom and
aunts

I'm sorry that I don't pay attention to every single
detail even when it should be obvious to me

I'm sorry that there isn't much I can afford

That I am so sensitive and fragile

That I don't inspire you to be deemed deserving of
a bouquet of flowers or set up spontaneous dates

I'm sorry I cannot pretend that I am okay when I
am not

I'm sorry i'm insecure

I'm sorry i cant be every woman you lay your eyes
on with burning desire

I do wish I could be them, so you'd want me no
matter where you look

Or where your mind wanders off to

And I'm sorry that I never will be

Tomb

The ghost of you lives inside my head

It's not that you're dead

But every house needs light

And the thought of you ignites

My abandoned dome of echoes and cold nights

My Love

I know

I'm not the woman of your dreams

Or perhaps the woman that you thought I'd be

It seems my image fills your eyes' appetite

There's no room for my flaws

Your atmosphere rejects my sensitivity

It's true what they say

Beauty fades

But the inside remains

I've concluded that I am bland

I'm currently inconvenienced by what is out of my
control, constellations on my face

You prefer your imagination over my scent

You prefer your hand over my body

I know

You think I'm lazy

I lack excitement and barely teach you anything

Unlike your colleague, who's…amazing

It isn't fair, you know

It isn't fair for me to compare myself with her

She has far more experience

Far more enthusiasm

Much more life and brilliance

I suspect you'd be happier with someone like her

Cause what is it that I can give you?

Nothing

I hear your silent thoughts

Your secret comments

I can taste your disappointment when you expect
something from me

My love

My soul begs for you to be quenched

Your eyes have wandered

And found their match

I am not your happiness my love

I know

Favorite color

My favorite color?

My favorite color is the silent period on Sundays

When the earth takes a deep breath and smiles

Ready to take her rest

Like a middle aged woman excited to sip her tea
and read a book

My favorite color is when the atmosphere hugs us

And for a second, the sky paints a portrait for us

Kissing our foreheads and brushing the trees

My favorite color is a clear night sky while we
collectively prepare for the new week indoors

And you can hear the stars twinkling their lullabies

My favorite color is a sleeping baby's snuggles and
paced breathing

It's the dancing birds that raced us to the
awakening of a new day

See my favorite color isn't necessarily solid

It's silently breath-taking

And satiates all senses

A portrait you can smell

It's a memory you can tough

A desire you can live in

A utopia based on reality

My favorite color is Godly

Museum

May I show you something?

"Crushed marbles

Scattered crystals

Pale dust misty windows

Dented joy

Fragments of hopelessness

Cracked kindness

Wisdom perturbed

Disorganized maturity

Tortured desires

Useless needs

Fractures gaze

Frightened youth

Limited passions

Longing blues"

Do you seem me now? Am I breathtaking?

Red Wine

They say that its typical for the woman to fall in
love first than it is the man

Or that the woman is the first to admit feelings

But no matter what's true

I fell in love with you first

And I fell in love with you entirely

I fell for the fact that you are an extremely detail
oriented person

That you have OCD and not everyone understands
that

I love the fact that you are a sucker for math

I love that you try to hide your fears

Your loud bursts of laughter

The little squint in your eye when you feel your ego
is threatened

I love how you tremble when you think that you´re
about to make a bad decision

Or that your reputation is at stake

I love how your fingers shake when you´re in deep
concentration

And your left eyebrow twitches when you´re
focused on something´

I love how determined you are no matter how
tired, you always accomplish what you set your
mind to

I love your confidence

Even though that´s the one things that´s been
stabbing me ceaselessly

See you fell in love with me much later

While I was learning to let go and detach

But the problem was, even though I was detaching
I was still madly in love with you

You thought you felt the same but you were
interested and intrigued by what I could offer

And I was still in love with you even though what
you gave me was less than the bare minimum

You "loved" me because I was in your pocket

You had me in your hands

I was easy to handle

I caused no scenes and no problems

Quiet and in my corner

Ready for you when you called

Even though there were times I'd try to avoid you

The itch always won, and id call you

I'd call you to use me

But id also call you so I could love you

And so in our entanglement, we had a yin and
yang

One was loving

And the other conniving

You loved the idea or rather the fact that nobody
could have me but you

That I was only available for you whenever you
wanted

Because I looked at you as if you were the highest
of my standards

The best that I could do

But I was sharing you

I was sharing a tip of you

Because even half was too much

See I was in love with you

And you were in love with your power over me

Powerless

A constant smile is a foreign concept to my lips

Surely it brings a warming feeling to others

Because to me it only brings tears

Perhaps I am an opposite

An absurd contrast

But somehow that makes me special

I don't think I'm special

Isn't that a self-centered mindset?

Now tell me, society, who shall I be?

Selfish or altruistic

The former takes advantage of others

While the latter is taken advantage of

Have I evolved?

It seems the same weaknesses surround me

Just in grown vessels and heightened intelligence

Sincerity

I visited a forest once

In which the trees would bend themselves to make
for bridges

The grass would turn brown to not intimidate

The leaves would fade instead of whistle

So as to not create a scenery

The waterfall would dry to not seem abundant

The animals remained in caves to lock up their
beauty

Clouds would form but the rain wouldn't dare fall

To not show that the sky is alive

Lightning would strike the land constantly

To leave a mark and help the abuser

The weeds were tall to eliminate any chance of
admiration

Abandoned to its natural disaster

And it leaves me to wonder

Do I even love myself?

Drown

You say I won't tell you anything.

That I'm just silent

But can't you see how shallow my eyes get

when you seem upset?

Don't you hear my heart race when the tone

Does your voice become harsh?

Or how my hands shake when I want to

tell you something serious?

Do you hear how low my voice gets when I say

"everything is fine"?

Do you at least notice the different volumes of the

my silence?

My silence was already so loud for you to
understand

that I was scarred?

Didn't you notice my self-harm?:

Too happy, smiling too much, not taking care of

myself, isolating myself, extreme silence

Do you remember how I was when you tried to get

me

to conquer?

Do you still look at me like that?

Do you notice when I isolate myself?

When I don't send you a good message

day, you can't hear me begging for

send a good morning message?

Don't make me jealous when I look at the

flowers with desire

Why do you make me question if I look beautiful?

Why do you only tell me I look "pretty" when

did we miraculously come out?

Baby, do you even know me?

Can you understand me?

In fact, do you still want to understand me?

Have you ever thought about spoiling me?

Sometimes I want you to give me a massage

without needing to ask

But I don't ask, because you would have already
done it if

you wanted

And I don't want to make you do things that you

don't want to do

Nobody is perfect

But the way you admire other women

Makes me question if this is true

That doesn't mean I need you to feel

well with myself

But I'm with you

And your affirmation is a source of motivation

But now that I reflect

I'm probably not your motivation

Dear

You don't like me anymore

You don't even care about me anymore

I never thought you'd be the one to prove it to me

That "men are all equal"

That "men don't know what they want"

And it's funny how much it impacted me

Because you were my friend

You looked at me with a sparkle in your eyes

You cared so much about me

But now another woman has caught his eye

And she also has a boyfriend

So what does she have

That made you decide that I'm no longer your
muse

I was on a pedestal when I had your friendship

But I'm wondering if maybe that friendship was

just in my imagination

Because I didn't give you what you wanted

But she can't either

I even changed to be more like her

I made my voice softer

I became more mega

I just don't have my own business

And even with these changes

You never called or sent a message

But you are always spoiling him with your
attention and

gifts

But I should have realized

There's no point in trying to be like her

No one is like her

And maybe I should remember that the problem is
me

Because I should be happy alone

Without the help of someone else's attention

I guess you were never real

Just a fragment of my imagination

And I learned my lesson

I'm not a happy woman

Thank you, my dear

About the author

Marinela Domingos is a young Angolan graduate from the University of South Africa with a degree in International Relations and Diplomacy.

From a young age, she's had a great interest in literature and wrote her first unpublished book at the age of 13.

Marinela has never been ordinary, quite the opposite and this is evident in her style of writing, which is unique to her character. She dabbles in metaphors to paint a picture and convey intense feelings to the reader, making it difficult to know whether she is speaking from personal experience or whether her imagination took her down a path less traveled.

Her inspirations range from authors such as Anais Nin, Charles Bukowski, Henry Miller and Jean-Jaques Rousseau.

This will not be the last of her writing, she will return with more puns and ironies.